In The Year 1917

By

Kerry Butters

Contents

In The Year 1917

Timeline
January

Jan 10 The Allied Governments respond to US President Woodrow Wilson's December 1916 note, giving their terms for ending the war
Jan 10 Suffragettes the "Silent Sentinels" 1st protest outside The White House,in Washington led by Alice Paul and the National Woman's Party

Jan 11 Guy Bolton & PG Wodehouse's "Have a Heart" premieres in New York

Jan 13 Ammunitions ship explosion at Ekonomiia port near Archangel, Russia kills many and injures hundreds

Jan 16 The Greek Government accepts reparations for Allied losses sustained in recent actions in Greece
Jan 16 "Zimmermann Telegram" is sent from Germany to Mexico, stating in the event of the US entering World War I on the allied side, Mexico would be given Texas, Arizona and New Mexico. Intercepted by British intelligence and partially deciphered by the next day. It's release in March shifts US public opinion in favor of war against Germany.

Jan 17 US pays Denmark $25 million for Virgin Islands

Jan 19 The Silvertown explosion: 73 die when a munitions factory in Essex explodes.

Jan 27 Coen de Koning wins 2nd official 11 cities race (9:53) (record)

Jan 28 Municipally owned streetcars take to the streets of San Francisco, California

Jan 29 British submarine K13 sank in Gaire Loch, Scotland; 32 of her crew died

Jan 31 Germany notifies US that U-boats will attack neutral merchant ship

Jan 31 Mexican President Carranza announces a new constitution with many liberal elements; most of which his regime will not implement

February

Feb 1 German Großadmiral Alfred von Tirpitz announces unlimited submarine war

Feb 3 US liner Housatonic is sunk by German submarine, on the same day that US President Woodrow Wilson breaks off diplomatic relations with Germany

Feb 4 Belgian Council of Flanders established

Feb 5 Congress overrides Wilson's veto, curtailing Asian immigration

Feb 5 Morosco Theater opens at 217 W 45th St NYC (demolished 1982)

Feb 5 The last of the American troops commanded by General John Pershing leave Mexico; President Carranza will be assassinated within the next year

Feb 10 Johanna Westerdijk installed as the Netherlands' 1st female professor

Feb 15 San Francisco Public Library (Main Branch at Civic center) dedicated

Feb 16 1st synagogue in 425 years opens in Madrid

Feb 17 In Australia, Nationalist Party takes over a coalition government

Feb 18 1st major strike of the Russian "February Revolution" starts at the giant Putilov factory in Petrograd

Feb 20 Jerome Kern, Guy Bolton & P.G. Wodehouse's musical "Oh, Boy!" premieres in New York

Feb 21 British troopship SS Mendi sinks off Isle of Wight, 646 die
Feb 21 Train near Chirurcha, Romania, catches fire & explodes; hundreds die

Feb 22 German Navy torpedoes 7 Dutch ships

Feb 24 German plan to get Mexican help in WW I exposed (Zimmerman telegram)
Feb 24 Red Sox sell Smokey Joe Wood, his arm dead at 26, to Cleve for $15,000

Feb 26 1st jazz records recorded - "Dixie Jazz Band One Step" and "Livery Stable Blues" by Original Dixieland Jass Band for the Victor Talking Machine Company
Feb 26 Russian February Revolution: Tsar Nicolas II orders army to quell civil unrest in Petrograd - army mutinies
Feb 26 1st Annual fair at Utrecht Harbor (Netherlands)

Feb 28 AP reports Mexico & Japan will allie with Germany if US enters WW I

March
Mar 1 1st federal land bank chartered in USA
Mar 1 US government releases the plain text of the "Zimmermann Telegram" to the public

Mar 2 Jones Act: Puerto Rico territory created, US citizenship granted

Mar 3 US Congress passes 1st excess profits tax on corporations
Mar 3 1st major strike of the Russian "February Revolution" starts at the giant Putilov factory in Petrograd
Mar 3 Mexico and the USA renew diplomatic relations

Mar 3 German Foreign Secretary Arthur Zimmermann publicly admits the "Zimmermann Telegram" is genuine. Generates support for the US declaration of war on Germany in April.

Mar 5 US President Woodrow Wilson is inaugurated for a second term

Mar 7 1st jazz record record released on a 78 by Original Dixieland Jass Band for the Victor Talking Machine Company ("Dixie Jazz Band One Step," one side "Livery Stable Blues" other)

Mar 8 Russian "February Revolution" begins in earnest with protests celebrating International Woman's Day and riots in St Petersburg over food rations and conduct of the war

Mar 10 Batangas was formally founded as one of the Philippines's earliest encomiendas

Mar 11 1st NHL championship game ever played, Toronto Arenas beats Montreal Canadiens 7-3 in 1st of 2 game set (second game on March 13)
Mar 11 British forces occupy Baghdad, the capital of Mesopotamia, after Turkish forces evacuated

Mar 12 Russian Duma sets up the Provisional Committee; Soviets form Executive Committee
Mar 12 Stalin, Kamenev & Muranov arrive in Petrograd (St Petersburg)
Mar 12 A German submarine sinks an unamred US merchant ship, the 'Algonquin' on the same day that US President Woodrow Wilson gives executive order to arm US merchant ships

Mar 15 Nicholas II, the last Russian Tsar abdicates and nominates his brother Grand Duke Michael to succeed him

Mar 16 Russian Grand Duke Michael, brother of Tsar Nicholas II declines the Russian throne

Mar 17 1st exclusively women's bowling tournament begins in St Louis
Mar 17 Delta Phi Epsilon is founded at New York University Law School
Mar 17 Albert Anastasia is convicted of murdering longshoreman George Turino

Mar 19 US Supreme Court uphoelds 8-hr work day for railroad employees

Mar 20 After the sinking of 3 more American merchant ships, US President Woodrow Wilson meets with cabinet, who agree that war is inevitable

Mar 21 Loretta Walsh becomes US Navy's 1st female Petty Officer

Mar 22 The USA is the first nation to recognize the new government of Russia

Mar 23 Tornadoes kills 211 over 4 days in Midwest US

Mar 25 Canadian ace Billy Bishop claims his first victory, shooting down and mortally wounding German Leutnant Theiller

Mar 26 Stanley Cup: Seattle Metropolitans (PCHA) beat Montreal Canadiens (NHL), 3 games to 1 Seattle is 1st US team to win Stanley Cup
Mar 26 British win a battle against Turks at Gaza

Mar 28 Jews are expelled from Tel Aviv & Jaffa by Turkish authorities
Mar 28 Puccini's "La Rondine" premieres in Monte Carlo

Mar 31 US purchases Danish West Indies for $25M & renames them Virgin Islands

April

Apr 2 Jeannette Rankin (Rep-R-Mont) begins her term as 1st woman member of US House of Reps

Apr 2 US President Woodrow Wilson asks Congress to declare war against Germany

Apr 3 Vladimir Lenin arrives in Petrograd from Switzerland

Apr 3 Alfred Stieglitz opens 1st one-person show of Georgia O'Keeffee's work at 291 art gallery in New York

Apr 4 US Senate agrees (82-6) to participate in WWI

Apr 6 US declares war on Germany, enters World War I

Apr 7 De Falla's ballet "El Sombrero de tres Picos" premieres in Madrid

Apr 7 James Barries' "Old Lady Shows Her" premieres in London

Apr 9 Battle of Arras begins

Apr 9 Vimy Ridge in France stormed by Canadian troops

Apr 10 Munition factory explosion at Eddystone, Pennsylvania, kills 133 workers

Apr 11 Babe Ruth beats NY Yanks, pitching 3-hit 10-3 win for Red Sox

Apr 12 Bijou Theater opens at 222 W 45th St NYC (Demolished 1982)

Apr 12 Domenico Scarlatti & Jeab Cocteaus ballet premieres in Rome

Apr 14 Chicago White Sox Ed Cicotte no-hits St Louis Browns, 11-0

Apr 16 Lenin arrives back from exile in Russia at Finland Station, Petrograd to join the Russian Revolution

Apr 16 Vladimir Lenin issues his radical "April Theses" calling for Soviets to take power during the Russian Revolution

Apr 19 21st Boston Marathon won by Bill Kennedy of NY in 2:28:37.2

Apr 24 Yankee lefty George Mogridge no-hits Red Sox 2-1 at Fenway
Apr 24 US Congress passes the Liberty Loan Act, authorizing the
Treasury to issue a public subscription for 2 billion in bonds for the war

May
May 2 Cin Fred Tooney & Chic's Hippo Vaughn pitch duel no-hitter,
Vaughn gives up 2 hits & a run in 10th, so Cin wins 1-0

May 3 1st performance of Ernest Bloch's symphony "Israel"

May 4 A flotilla of US destroyer ships arrive in Queenstown, Ireland, to
aid in convoying ships to England

May 5 St Louis Brown Ernie Koob no-hits Chicago White Sox, 1-0

May 6 St Louis Brown Bob Groom no-hits Chicago White Sox, 3-0

May 7 Red Sox Babe Ruth beats Washington Senator Walter Johnson, 1-
0

May 10 Atlantic ships get destroyer escorts to stop German attacks

May 11 King George V grants Royal Letters Patent to New Zealand

May 12 42nd Preakness: E Haynes aboard Kalitan wins in 1:54.4
May 12 43rd Kentucky Derby: Charles Borel on Omar Khayyam wins in
2:04.6

May 13 1st appearance of Mary to 3 shepherd children in Fatima,
Portugal
May 13 Ernest Bloch's "Schelomo" premieres

May 15 The first officer's training camp is opened in the US, as the country prepares for war

May 18 Satie/Massine/Picasso's ballet "Parade" premieres in Paris
May 18 US Congress passes Selective Service Act, authorizing the federal government to raise a national army for the American entry into World War I through compulsory enlistment
May 18 First units of the American Expeditionary Force, commanded by General John J. Pershing, is ordered to France

May 20 Turkish government authorizes Jews to return to Tel Aviv & Jaffa

May 21 Leo Pinckney, 1st American drafted during WW I
May 21 The Great Fire of Atlanta: at least 10,000 people were displaced, but there was only one fatality

May 23 Dutch 2nd Chamber approves 1908 conscription draft

May 26 Walt Cruise hit 1st HR out of Braves Field

May 27 Race riot in East St Louis Illinois, 1 black killed

May 30 Jazz standard "Dark Town Strutters Ball" by Original Dixieland Jass Band first recorded

June
Jun 1 Hank Gowdy is 1st baseball player to enlist during WW I

Jun 2 Canadian ace Billy Bishop undertakes a solo mission behind enemy lines, shooting down three aircrafts as they were about to take off and several more on the ground, for which he is awarded the Victoria Cross

Jun 4 1st Pulitzer prize awarded to Richards & Elliott (Julia Ward Howe)

Jun 4 American men begin registering for the draft

Jun 4 Most Excellent Order of British Empire inaugurated by King George V to recognise the efforts of his people in WWI

Jun 5 10 million US men begin registering for draft in WW I

Jun 7 Melvin Jones and a number of other Chicago businessmen found Lions Clubs International, now the largest service organization in the world

Jun 7 The British detonate mines beneath the German-held Messines Ridge, in the Ypres area

Jun 8 Walt Disney graduates from Benton High School

Jun 10 60,000 people of Petrograd Russia welcome Prince Kropotkin (banned 41 years) returning after February Russian Revolution

Jun 10 Limburgse mine workers strike

Jun 11 King Alexander assumes the throne of Greece after his father Constantine I abdicated under pressure by allied armies occupying Athens.

Jun 12 US Secret Service extends protection of the President to include his family

Jun 13 World War I: the deadliest German air raid on London during World War I is carried out by Gotha G bombers and results in 162 deaths, including 46 children, and 432 injuries.

Jun 14 1st German air attack on England, 100+ killed in East London

Jun 14 Gen Pershing & his HQ staff arrived in Paris during WW I

Jun 15 In order to calm troubled relations with Ireland, the British grant amnesty to the Prisoners taken during the Easter Rising of 1916

Jun 16 1st All Russian Congress of the Soviets convenes in Petrograd, Russia

Jun 16 49th Belmont: James Butwell aboard Hourless wins in 2:17.8

Jun 19 The British Royal Family, which has had strong German ties since George I, renounces its German names and titles and adopts the name of Windsor

Jun 21 Hawaiian Red Cross forms

Jun 23 Ammunition factory in Boleweg Bohemia explodes, killing 1,000
Jun 23 Ernie Shore replaces Red Sox pitcher Babe Ruth with a runner on, he throws him out & retires all 26 he faces for a perfect game
Jun 23 31st U.S. Women's National Championship: Molla Bjurstedt beats Marion Vanderhoef (4-6, 6-0, 6-2)

Jun 24 Russian Black Sea fleet mutinies at Sebastopol

Jun 26 1st US Expeditionary Force arrives in France during World War I

Jun 27 1st baseball player (Hank Gowdy) to enter WW I military service
Jun 27 Venizelos takes over as Prime Minister of Greece and severs relations with Central Powers, bringing Greece onside with the Allies in WWI

Jun 28 Potato entrepreneurs begins in Amsterdam

July
Jul 1 257cm-mirror for Mount Wilson Observatory mountedJul 1 Race riots in East St Louis Illinois (40 to 200 reported killed)
Jul 1 Reds' Fred Toney pitches completes doubleheader victories over Pirates
Jul 1 Robins (Dodgers) play their 1st Sunday game in Brooklyn

Jul 2 Riots in East St Louis Mo

Jul 3 Spontaneous demonstration at Tauride Palace, Petrograd

Jul 6 T. E. Lawrence captures port of Aqaba from Turks

Jul 9 British battleship HMS Vanguard explodes at Scapa Flow (the result of an internal explosion of faulty cordite), killing 804

Jul 10 Emma Goldman imprisoned for obstructing draft

Jul 12 The Bisbee Deportation occurs as vigilantes kidnap and deport nearly 1,300 striking miners and others from Bisbee, Arizona.

Jul 13 Vision of Virgin Mary appeared to children of Fatima, Portugal

Jul 17 Royal Proclamation by King George V changes name of British Royal family from German Saxe-Coburg-Gotha to Windsor
Jul 20 Pact of Corfu signed: Serbs, Croats & Slovenes form Yugoslavia
Jul 20 WW I draft lottery held; #258 is 1st drawn

Jul 21 Russian Revolution: Socialist Alexander Kerensky becomes Russian Prime Minister

Jul 22 British bomb German lines at Ypres, 4,250,000 grenades

Jul 23 Cleveland Metropolitan Park District establishes

Jul 25 Sir Thomas Whyte introduces the first income tax in Canada as a "temporary" measure (lowest bracket is 4% and highest is 25%).

Jul 26 J. Edgar Hoover gets job in US Department of Justice

Jul 27 World War I: Allied troops reach the Yser Canal in the prelude to the Battle of Passchendaele

Jul 28 Silent Parade organised by James Weldon Johnson of 10,000 African-Americans who march on 5th Ave in NYC to protest against lynching

Jul 30 Board of Commissioners of Cleveland Metroparks has its 1st meeting

Jul 31 3rd battle of Ypres begins

August
Aug 1 Frank Little, IWW organizer, lynched in Butte, MT

Aug 4 Pravda calls for the killing of all capitalists, priests & officers

Aug 5 British troops attack canal of Ypres in Boesinghe, Belgium
Aug 5 The entire US National Guard is taken into national service, subject to presidential rather than state control

Aug 6 World War I: Battle of Mărăşeşti between the Romanian and German armies begins.

Aug 9 Canadian Parliament passes the Compulsory Military Act which is opposed by many French-Canadians from Québec

Aug 13 Phillies steal 5 bases in an inning against Braves
Aug 13 A revolt in Catalonia, the province in northeast Spain that has long seen itself as independent.

Aug 14 China declares war on Germany & Austria

Aug 14 Leeuwen soccer team forms

Aug 17 Italy declares war on Turkey

Aug 18 Dutch Naval Air Force forms (MLD)

Aug 18 A Great Fire in Thessaloniki, Greece destroys 32% of the city leaving 70,000 individuals homeless.

Aug 19 Sunday benefit baseball game at Polo Grounds results in John McGraw & Christy Mathewson's arrest for violating Blue laws

Aug 22 Pittsburgh Pirates play 4th straight extra inning game, Carson Bigbee sets record of 11 at-bats, they lose in 22 innings to Dodgers

Aug 23 Race riot in Houston Texas (2 blacks & 11 whites killed)

Aug 25 37th U.S. Men's National Championship: Robert Lindley Murray beats Nathaniel W. Niles (5-7, 8-6, 6-3, 6-3)

Aug 27 Indians set club record by stealing eight bases in a game

Aug 28 Ten suffragists arrested as they picket the White House

Aug 31 In China, Sun Yat-sen and his supporters' 'rump' parliament establishes a military government and elects Sun Yat-sen as commander-in-Chief

September
Sep 2 Deutsche Vaterlands Partei formed by admiral Tirpitz

Sep 3 1st night bombing of London by German aircraft
Sep 3 German troops overrun Riga, Latvia
Sep 3 Grover Cleveland Alexander pitches complete wins in a doubleheader
Sep 3 Utrecht soccer team Holland forms

Sep 6 French pilot Georges Guynemer shoots down 54th German aircraft

Sep 15 Russia proclaimed a republic by Alexander Kerensky's Provisional government

Sep 17 Honus Wagner, retires at 43, Pirates retire his #33

Sep 20 British assault on Polygon Forest, France
Sep 20 Paraguay becomes a signatory to the Buenos Aires copyright treaty.

Sep 26 British assault on Menin-street, France

Sep 27 Broadhurst Theater opens at 235 W 44th St NYC
Sep 27 EHC soccer team forms in Hoensbroek Neth

October
Oct 4 British assault on Broodseinde, France

Oct 6 Battle of Passchendaele: Canadian troops capture the village of Passchendaele in the Third Battle of Ypres, after 250,000 casualties on both sides

Oct 8 Leon Trotsky named chairman of the Petrograd Soviet as Bolsheviks gain control

Oct 10 Plymouth Theater opens at 236 W 45th St NYC

Oct 13 Soviets accept establishment of Petrograd Military
Oct 13 7th College Football Crab Bowl Classic: Navy beats Maryland 62-0 in Annapolis

Oct 15 Chicago White Sox beat NY Giants, 4 games to 2 in 14th World Series
Oct 15 Dutch dancer Mata Hari is executed by firing squad for spying for Germany during WWI at Vincennes near Paris

Oct 17 1st British bombing of Germany

Oct 19 Love Field in Dallas, Texas, is opened

Oct 20 US suffragette Alice Paul begins a 7 month jail sentence for protesting women's rights in Washington

Oct 21 1st Americans to see action on front lines of WWI: US troops enter front lines at Sommervillier under French command
Oct 21 Petrograds garrison accepts Revolutionary Military Committee

Oct 23 1st Infantry division "Big Red One" shoots 1st US shot in WW I
Oct 23 Lenin speaks against Kamenev, Kollontai, Stalin & Trotsky

Oct 24 Battle at Caporetto: German & Austria smash Italian army

Oct 25 Pan-Russian Congress opens in Petrograd

Oct 26 Petrograd Soviet accepts establishment of Military
Oct 26 World War I: Brazil declared in state of war with Central Powers.

Oct 27 20,000 women march in a suffrage parade in New York, US

Oct 30 British government gives final approval to Balfour Declaration

Oct 31 Eugene O'Neill's "In the Zone" premieres in NYC
Oct 31 World War I: Battle of Beersheba in southern Palestine - "last successful cavalry charge in history" performed by the 4th Australian Light Horse

November
Nov 2 In WWI the 1st US soldiers are killed in combat: James Gresham, Thomas Enright and Merle Hay
Nov 2 Balfour Declaration proclaims support for a Jewish state in Palestine

Nov 2 Lansing-Ishii Agreement; US recognizes Japan's privileges in China

Nov 3 1st class US mail now costs 3 cents per ounce

Nov 5 Gen Pershing & US troops see action on Western Front for 1st time
Nov 5 Supreme Court decision (Buchanan v Warley) strikes down Louisville, Kentucky, ordinance requiring backs & whites to live in separate areas

Nov 6 Bolshevik revolution begins with bombardment of the Winter Palace in Petrograd during the Russian October Revolution
Nov 6 New York State adopts a constitutional amendment giving women the right to vote in state elections

Nov 7 British capture Gaza, Palestine, from Turks
Nov 7 October Revolution in Russia; Lenin and the Bolsheviks seize power, capture the Winter Palace and overthrow the Provisional Government.

Nov 8 People's Commissars gives authority to Lenin, Trotsky & Stalin during October Revolution
Nov 8 Telephone Co runs 1st advertisement for Army operators, receives 7,000 applicants

Nov 10 41 suffragists are arrested in front of White House
Nov 10 Faure's 2nd Violo Sonate premieres
Nov 10 New bolshevik government under Lenin suspends freedom of press (temporary) during October Revolution

Nov 16 British occupy Tel Aviv and Jaffa

Nov 17 Lenin defends "temporary" removal of freedom of the press

Nov 18 Sigma Alpha Rho, a Jewish high school fraternity, is founded in Philadelphia, Pennsylvania.

Nov 20 First successful tank use in battle (Britain breaks through German lines) at Battle of Cambrai WWI
Nov 20 Ukrainian Republic declared

Nov 21 Maxim Gorky calls Vladimir Lenin a blind fanatic and unthinking adventurer

Nov 24 Nine police officers and one civilian are killed when a bomb explodes at the Milwaukee, Wisconsin police headquarters building.

Nov 26 NHL forms with Montreal Canadiens, Montreal Maroons, Toronto Arenas, Ottawa Senators & Quebec Bulldogs; National Hockey Association disbands
Nov 26 The new government of Russia offers an armistice to Germany and Austria-Hungary

Nov 28 Sigmund Romberg's revue "Over the Top" premieres in NYC

Nov 29 A Supreme Allied War Council meets at Versailles to define war aims

December
Dec 1 Boys Town founded by Father Edward Flanagan west of Omaha, Nebraska

Dec 2 Han Yong-woon, found Zen awakening at Osean Monastery Korea

Dec 3 After nearly 20 years of planning and construction, the Quebec Bridge opens to traffic.
Dec 3 The Supreme Allied War Council, meeting at Versailles to define war aim, fails to reach an agreement

Dec 5 Austro-German Forces launch an offensive against the Italians on the western end of their line, around Asiago

Dec 6 French munition ship "Mont Blanc" explodes in Halifax, kills 1,700
Dec 6 Taking advantage of the temporary relaxation of authority in Russia, Finland declares itself a republic, following the Ukraine on 20 November

Dec 7 US becomes 13th country to declare war on Austria during World War I
Dec 7 The USA's 42nd 'Rainbow' Division arrives in France (with Colonel Douglass MacArthur among its ranks)

Dec 9 British forces under General Allenby capture Jerusalem

Dec 11 13 black soldiers hanged for participation in Houston riot
Dec 11 German-occupied Lithuania proclaims independence from Russia

Dec 12 French troop train derails in French Alps killing 543
Dec 12 Rev Edward Flanagan forms Boys Town outside Omaha, Nebraska

Dec 14 UFA, Universal Film AG, forms in Germany

Dec 15 Moldavian Republic declares independence from Russia
Dec 15 World War I: An armistice is reached between the new Russian Bolshevik government and the Central Powers.

Dec 18 Soviet regiment (Stalin/Lenin) declares Finland Independent
Dec 18 The 18th Amendment, authorizing prohibition of alcohol, is approved by the US congress and sent to the states for ratification

Dec 19 1st NHL game played on artificial ice in Toronto
Dec 19 Quebec Bulldogs play their 1st professional hockey game

Dec 20 Cheka formed - Soviet state security force and forerunner to the KGB, under Felix Dzerzhinsky after decree by Lenin
Dec 20 A second nationwide referendum on military conscription is rejected by the Australian public

Dec 22 Flanders declares its independence, under Pieter Tack

Dec 23 3 British warships come close to Holland

Dec 25 "Why Marry" 1st drama to win Pulitzer Prize, premieres in NYC
Dec 25 Louis Hirsch and Otto Harbach's musical "Going Up" premieres in New York City

Dec 26 1st NHL defensemen to score a goal: Toronto Maple Leaf Harry Cameron
Dec 26 US Federal government took over operation of American railroads for duration of WW I

Dec 30 -32°F (-36°C) in Mountain City, Tennessee (state record)
Dec 30 -37°F (-38°C) in Lewisburg, WV (state record)

Dec 31 Dutch Social-democratic trade union NVV counts 159,450 members

1917 Fun Facts

David Lloyd George was prime minister.

King George V was in power.

The average house cost £195, which in today's money is £15,249.

The average salary was £101, which equates to £7,901 today.

The average car would set you back £250 in 1917. This would be £19,950 in today's money.

America entered World War One on April 6.

Silvertown explosion - a blast at a munitions factory in London killed 73 and injured more than 400.

The Russian Revolution took place.

A litre of fuel was 4p, which in today's money is £3.08.

Ten suffragists were arrested at the White House on August, 28.

Winston Churchill was appointed Minister of Munitions.

It took five days to get from London to New York and three and a half months to travel from London to Australia.

New York State allowed women to vote on November, 6.

A Boeing aircraft flew for the first time on June 15.

America paid Denmark $25 million for the Virgin Islands.

British battleship HMS Vanguard explodes at Scapa Flow, killing 804 on July 9.

Hit song, Over There by Nora Bayes, was released before going on to be the most popular song in the First World War

The Ford Model T was the most popular car in 1917.

Cleopatra was the best selling film that year.

Fuel for cars was sold in drug stores only.

Only 14 percent of the homes had a bathtub.

Only 8 percent of the homes had a telephone.

The maximum speed limit in most cities was 10 mph.

The tallest structure in the world was the Eiffel Tower.

Childrens Toys

Despite the ongoing war, the lives of children throughout December were still centred around excitement for what Santa Claus would bring them on Christmas morning.
Like television adverts today, children were bombarded with toy and present ideas in print form in papers and magazines in the run up to Christmas.

TOP TEN TOYS OF 1917

1.Teddy Bear
2.Erector Set (Meccano)
3.Lionel Trains (
4.Lincoln Logs
5.Raggedy Ann Doll

6.Radio Flyer Wagon
7.Tinker Toys
8.Crayola Crayons 8 pack
9.Tin Toys
10.Tiddlywinks

Other popular toys included: Snap Card Game, Playing cards,
marbles, checkers, chess, yoyos, wooden tops, Baseball Cards Ping Pong
Jigsaw Puzzles
and dolls.

Famous Births
January

Jan 1 Jule Gregory Charney, American meteorologist (d. 1981)
Jan 1 Albert Mol, Dutch actor (d. 2004)

Jan 2 Vera Zorina, German dancer (d. 2003)

Jan 3 Vernon A. Walters, American diplomat and US permanent rep to
the UN (1989-91), born in NYC, New York (d. 2002)
Jan 3 Roger W. Straus, Jr., American publisher (d. 2004)

Jan 4 Maurice Wohl, English broker/multi-millionaire

Jan 5 Reginald Smith Brindle, composer
Jan 5 Wieland Wagner, German opera director
Jan 5 Jane Wyman, American actress (Magnificent Obsession) and 1st
wife of Ronald Reagan, born in Saint Joseph, Missouri (d. 2007)
Jan 5 Francis L. Kellogg, U.S. diplomat and prominent socialite (d.
2006)

Jan 6 Guillermo Rosario, Dutch Antilles, writer (E rais ku no ke muri)
Jan 6 Koo Chen-fu, Chinese negotiator (d. 2005)

Jan 7 Ulysses Sipmson Kay, composer

Jan 8 Peter Taylor, US writer
Jan 8 Stanley Prager, American comedian (College Bowl), born in NYC, New York

Jan 9 Herbert Lom, Czech, actor (Pink Panther Strikes Again, Dorian Gray)

Jan 10 Jerry Wexler, music producer (Aretha Franklin/Bob Dylan)

Jan 12 Walter Hendl, West New York NJ, conductor
Jan 12 Jimmy Skinner, Canadian hockey coach (d. 2007)
Jan 12 Maharishi Mahesh Yogi, Indian spiritualist (d. 2008)

Jan 13 Felix Guerro Diaz, composer

Jan 16 Buddy Lester, actor (Nick-Phil Silvers Show), born in Chicago, Illinois
Jan 16 Carl Karcher, founded the Carl's Jr. hamburger chain (d. 2008)

Jan 17 Maruthur Gopalan Ramachandran, (MGR), Indian film star, politician
Jan 17 Oskar Morawetz, Svetla Czechoslovakia, composer
Jan 17 Ulyses Simpson Kay, composer
Jan 17 Ramón Cardemil, Chilean huaso (d. 2007)

Jan 18 Oscar Lewenstein, impressario
Jan 18 Wang Yung-ching, Taiwanese businessman

Jan 19 John Raitt, Bonnie Raitt's father/singer/actor (Pajama Game)
Jan 19 Rudolf Maros, composer

Jan 21 Rohan Butler, historian

Jan 22 Albert "Pud" Brown, clarinetist/saxophonist

Jan 22 Herwig Hensen, [Flor Mielants], Flemish poet/playwright

Jan 24 Ernest Borgnine, actor (Ice Station Zebra, McHale's Navy, Marty), (d. 2012), born in Hamden, Connecticut (d. 2012)

Jan 25 Ilya Prigogine, Russian scientist Nobel Laureate (d. 2003)
Jan 25 Jânio Quadros, Brazilian politician (d. 1992)

Jan 29 John Raitt, actor/singer (Chevy Show, Pajama Game), born in Santa Ana, California

Jan 30 Paul Frère, Belgian racing driver and motorsport journalist d. 2008)

Jan 31 Erich Geiringer, general practitioner campaigner
Jan 31 José Maceda, Filipino composer, born in Manila, Philippines (d. 2004)

February
Feb 4 Aga Yahya Khan, Pakistan military/politician

Feb 6 Zsa Zsa Gabor [Zsa Sari], Hungarian-born actress (Queen of Outer Space), born in Budapest (d. 2016)
Feb 6 Arthur Gold, pianist, born in Toronto, Ontario
Feb 6 Liberato Firmino Sifonia, composer

Feb 11 Richard Jock Kinneir, graphic designer
Feb 11 Sidney Sheldon, American novelist and playwright (Master of the Game, Bloodline, The Bachelor and the Bobby Soxer), born in Chicago, Illinois (d. 2007)
Feb 11 T. Nagi Reddy, Indian revolutionary (d. 1976)

Feb 12 Thomas K Scherman, American conductor (Little Orch Society 1947-75), born in NYC, New York
Feb 12 Raizo Matsuno, Japanese politician (d. 2006)

Feb 13 Polly Rose, actress (Myrtle-Love That Jill)

Feb 14 Herbert A Hauptman, American x-ray crystallographer (Nobel 1985), born in NYC, New York

Feb 17 Abdur Rahman Badawi, Egyptian philosopher (d. 2002)
Feb 17 Guillermo González Camarena, Mexican inventor (d. 1965)

Feb 19 Dick Emery, actor (Yellow Submarine, Loot, Baby Love), born in London, England
Feb 19 Carson McCullers, American novelist (Heart Is a Lonely Hunter)

Feb 20 Frederick Page, CEO (British Aerospace Aircraft Group)

Feb 21 Victor G M Marijnen, Dutch premier (1963-65)

Feb 22 Harmen van Rossum, civil servant/resistance fighter (WWII)
Feb 22 Jack Robertson, cricketer (superb England batsman only played 11 Tests)
Feb 22 Jane Bowles, American writer, born in NYC, New York (d. 1973)

Feb 23 Kenneth Tobey, actor (Chuck-Whirlybirds) [or Mar 23]

Feb 24 William Fairbank, physicist (superconductivity), born in Minneapolis, Minnesota

Feb 25 Alex Gordon, Welsh architect, born in Ayr, Scotland
Feb 25 [John] Anthony Burgess [Wilson], essayist and novelist (A Clockwork Orange), born in Harpurhey, Lancashire (d. 1993)
Feb 25 Asta E R Elstak, Suriname/Dutch social worker

Feb 26 Robert Taft Jr.

Feb 27 John Connally, (Gov-D/R-Texas), shot in Kennedy motorcade

Feb 28 Hans Deutgen, Swedish world champion archer
Feb 28 John B Connally, (Gov/Sen-D/R-Tx), took a bullet with JFK

March

Mar 1 Dinah Shore, singer (See the USA in a Chevrolet), born in Winchester, Tennessee
Mar 1 Robert Lowell, American poet/pacifist (Lord Weary's Castle, Near the Ocean), born in Boston, Massachusetts

Mar 2 Desi Arnaz, Cuban-American actor (I Love Lucy), born in Santiago de Cuba (d. 1986)
Mar 2 Jim Konstanty, baseball player (NL MVP 1950)
Mar 2 John Gardner, composer
Mar 2 David Goodis, American writer (d. 1967)

Mar 3 Bert van Aerschot, Flemish writer (Elevator, Women)
Mar 3 Sameera Moussa, Egyptian nuclear scientist (d. 1952)

Mar 4 Clyde McCullough, American baseball player (d. 1982)

Mar 6 J A Mommersteeg, Dutch asst sect of Defense (KVP)
Mar 6 Roy Scott, cricketer (one Test NZ v England 1947, 18, 1-74)
Mar 6 Will Eisner, American illustrator and cartoonist (d. 2005)
Mar 6 Frankie Howerd, English comedian (d. 1992)

Mar 7 Davis Roberts, actor (Mr Johnson-Boone), born in Mobile, Alabama
Mar 7 Janet Collins, ballerina
Mar 7 Robert Erickson, composer

Mar 8 A Marja, [ATE Mooy], Dutch literary (Shreds on the River)

Mar 9 Dante B Fascell, (Rep-D-FL, 1955-)

Mar 10 Frank Perconte, American sergeant from Easy Company during WWII.

Mar 11 Robert L Carter, Caryville, Florida, American civil rights activist and judge (Brown v. Board of Education, NAACP v. Alabama) (d. 2012)

Mar 12 Googie Withers, actress (1 of Our Aircraft is Missing), born in Karachi, India
Mar 12 Tom Normanton, British MP

Mar 13 Ina Ray Hutton, orchestra leader (Ina Ray Hutton Show), born in Chicago, Illinois
Mar 13 Maria Vlamynck, Flemish author

Mar 14 Macha Louis Rosenthal, critic/poet

Mar 16 Samael Aun Weor, Colombian writer (d. 1977)

Mar 17 Arthur Basil Cotle, medievalist
Mar 17 Brian Boydell, composer

Mar 19 Dino Lipatti, composer
Mar 19 Laszlo Szabo, Hungarian chess player (d. 1998)

Mar 20 Dolf Verspoor, literary/interpreter (M Nijhoff Prize 1958)
Mar 20 Peter Caddy, founder (Findhorn Community)
Mar 20 Vera Lynn, singer (Anniversary Waltz)

Mar 21 Frank Hardy, Australian author (d. 1994)

Mar 22 Charles Pick, British publisher (William Heinemann), (d. 2000)
Mar 22 Virginia Grey, LA, actress (Another Thin Man, Idiot's Delight, Idaho)

Mar 23 H C Allen, American historian

Mar 23 Johnny Guarnieri, American jazz pianist (Morey Amsterdam Show), born in NYC, New York (d. 1985)
Mar 23 Kenneth Tobey, actor (The Thing, Strange Invaders) [or Feb 23]
Mar 23 Patricia Burke, actress (Forbidden), born in Milan, Italy

Mar 24 John Kendrew, British molecular biologist, Nobel laureate (d. 1997)
Mar 24 Constantine Andreou, Greek-Brazilian artist (d. 2007)

Mar 26 Jean Graham Hall, circuit court judge (England)
Mar 26 Rufus Thomas [Mr. Swing], American musician (Do the Funky Chicken), born in Cayce, Mississippi (d. 2001)

Mar 27 Cyrus Vance, US Secretary of State (1977-80), born in Clarksburg, West Virginia (d. 2002)
Mar 27 Harry West, Unionist party leader (Unionist)

Mar 29 Arthur Knight, CEO (Courtaulds)
Mar 29 Man o' War, American thoroughbred racehorse (winner of 20 out of 21 races & $249,465) (d. 1947)

Mar 30 Els Aarne, Estonian composer, born in Makiivka, Russian Empire (d. 1995)
Mar 30 Herbert Anderson, actor (Henry-Dennis The Menace)
Mar 30 Rudolf Bruci, composer

April
Apr 1 Johnny Andrews, singer/host (Songs at Twilight), born in Boston, Massachusetts
Apr 1 Leon Janney, actor (Hawk), born in Ogden, Utah

Apr 2 Dabbs Greer, actor (Gunsmoke, Little House on Prairie), born in Fairview, Missouri
Apr 2 Lou Monte, NJ, singer (Peppino the Italian Mouse)

Apr 3 Bill Finegan, (Sauter-Finegan Band, Sat Night Revue), born in Newark, New Jersey
Apr 3 Tibor Andrasovan, composer

Apr 4 Joseph Ortiz, French-Algerian extremist (barricade uprising)

Apr 5 Richard Yardumian, American composer (Come Creator Spirit), born in Philadelphia, Pennsylvania (d. 1985)
Apr 5 Robert [Albert] Bloch, American sci-fi author (Hugo, Psycho)

Apr 6 Julian Faber, CEO (Willis Faber)
Apr 6 Shakey, [Walter Horton], Miss, harmonicist (Everybody's Fishin')
Apr 6 Leonora Carrington, Clayton-le-Woods UK, British-Mexican Surrealist artist

Apr 7 R G Armstrong, actor (T.H.E. Cat), born in Birmingham, Alabama (d. 2012)

Apr 9 Johannes Bobrowski, writer
Apr 9 Vincent O'Brien, racehorse trainer
Apr 9 Brad Dexter, American actor (d. 2002)

Apr 10 Robert Burns Woodward, organic chemist (Nobel 1965)

Apr 11 Danny Gallivan, Canadian radio and television sportscaster (d. 1993)
Apr 11 David Westheimer, American novelist (d. 2005)

Apr 12 M Marie Wadlow, softball pitcher (Hall of Fame 1957), born in St Louis, Missouri (d. 1979)
Apr 12 Vinoo Mankad, cricketer (India's greatest all-rounder to his time)
Apr 12 Helen Forrest, American singer (d. 1999)

Apr 13 Howard Keel, American actor, singer and president of the Screen Actors Guild (7 Brides for 7 Brothers, Kiss Me Kate), born in Gillespie, Illinois (d. 2004)

Apr 14 Valerie Hobson, North Ireland, actress (Great Expectations)
Apr 14 Marvin Miller, American labor activist, (d. 2012)

Apr 15 Hans Conried, actor (Bullwinkle Show, Make Room for Daddy), born in Baltimore, Maryland
Apr 15 Pietro Grossi, composer

Apr 16 Barry Nelson, American actor, first actor to play James Bond, born in San Francisco, California (d. 2007)
Apr 16 Charlotte Salomon, German-Jewish artist, born in Berlin, Germany

Apr 17 Bill Clements, American politician

Apr 18 Louise Frederika, Queen of Greece
Apr 18 Ty LaForest, Canadian baseball player (d. 1947)

Apr 19 Johnny Hoes, Dutch musician/producer (Wished I'd stayed with my Mom)

Apr 21 Emanuel Vardi, Jerusalem Israel, violist, SD Symph 1978-82)

Apr 22 Leo Abse, Welsh politician and biographer, born in Cardiff (d. 2008)
Apr 22 Sidney Nolan, Australia, painter/illustrator (Ned Kelly)
Apr 22 Yvette Chauviré, French ballerina, born in Paris (d. 2016)

Apr 23 Jacob Kistemaker, nuclear physicist (ultra centrifuge)

Apr 25 Ella Fitzgerald, American jazz singer (Is it live or Memorex), born in Newport News, Virginia (d. 1996)

Apr 26 I. M. Pei, Chinese-American architect (1961 Brunner Prize), born in Guangzhou, China

Apr 26 Sal "The Barber" Maglie, pitcher (NY Giants, 8th best won-lost pct)

Apr 28 Joop Waasdorp, Dutch writer (Naked Life)

Apr 28 Robert Woodruff Anderson, New York, writer (Tea & Sympathy, Never Sang for My Father)

Apr 28 Robert Cornthwaite, St Helen Oregon, actor (Thing, War of the Worlds)

Apr 29 Celeste Holm, American actress (Gentleman's Agreement, All About Eve), born in NYC, New York (d. 2012)

Apr 29 Maya Deren (born Eleanora Derenkowskaia), American filmmaker , born in Kiev, Ukraine

Apr 30 Bea Wain, American singer and radio host (Deep Purple, Heart and Soul), born in The Bronx, Yew York (d. 2017)

May

May 1 Danielle Darrieux, French actress (Alexander the Great, Mayerling)

May 1 John Beradino, actor (Steve Hardy-General Hospital), born in Los Angeles, California

May 1 Louis G "Lo" van Hensbergen, actor/author (Amsterdam Affair)

May 1 Ahron Soloveichik, Orthodox Jewish rabbi, born in Khislavichi, Russia (d. 2001)

May 2 Albert Castelyns, Belgian water polo player and bobsledder

May 3 James Penberthy, composer

May 3 Betty Comden, American lyricist, (d. 2006)

May 3 Kiro Gligorov, Macedonia, President of the Republic of Macedonia 1991-1999 (d. 2012)

May 4 Edward Toner Cone, composer

May 5 Ron Saggers, cricket wicket-keeper (effective NSW & Aussie late 40's)

May 6 Kal Mann, American lyricist (d. 2001)

May 7 David Tomlinson, Scotland, actor (Mary Poppins, Helter Skelter)
May 7 William Geoffrey Biddle, bomb disposal expert

May 9 George Fleming, cyclist
May 9 John Arnatt, actor (Circumstantial Evidence)

May 11 Hon Montague Woodhouse, Greek resistance organiser

May 12 Andre A Rieu, Dutch conductor

May 13 Paul Osmond, British senior civil servant
May 13 Wilhelmus C Wijen, [Broeder Pius], social worker (Curacao)

May 14 Herta Ryder, literary agent
May 14 Lou Harrison, American composer (Rapunzel), born in Portland, Oregon

May 15 Hugh Edward Lance Falkus, filmmaker/naturalist

May 16 George Gaynes, actor (Tootsie, Police Academy), born in Helsinki Finland (d. 2016)
May 16 Geraint Jones, conductor/organist

May 18 Charles Wintour, journalist
May 18 James Donald, Aberdeen Scotland, actor (Bridge on River Kwai, Vikings)

May 20 Enyss Djemil, composer
May 20 Richard Cobb, British historian, born in Frinton-on-Sea (d. 1996)
May 20 Guy Favreau, French Canadian lawyer (d. 1967)
May 20 Bergur Sigurbjörnsson, Icelandic politician (d. 2005)

May 21 Dennis Day, Irish tenor/comedian (Jack Benny Show, Danny Boy)
May 21 Heather Swift, local councillor
May 21 Jean-Louis Curtis, French writer (Just Causes)
May 21 Raymond Burr, BC Canada, actor (Perry Mason, Ironsides, Godzilla)
May 21 Ronald John Bilsland Colville, businessman

May 22 Jean-Louis Laffitte Curtis, novelist
May 22 Georg Tintner, Austrian-born conductor (d. 1999)
May 22 Nathan Davis, American actor
May 22 Daniel Nagrin, American modern dancer and choreographer

May 23 Edward Norton Lorenz, American mathematician and meteorologist, born in West Hartford, Connecticut (d. 2008)

May 24 Derek Hodgson, British high court judge
May 24 Lord Campbell of Alloway, QC
May 24 Theodore Hesburgh, president (Notre Dame), born in Syracuse, New York

May 25 Jimmy Hamilton, saxophonist
May 25 Steve Cochran, Eureka CA, actor (Mozambique, Gay Senotiys, Dallas)

May 26 Eva Szorenyi, Hungarian actress, freedom activist for Hungary

May 28 Papa John Creach, Beaver Falls, Pennsylvania, American blues violinist (Hot Tuna, Jefferson Airplane)

May 28 Barry Commoner, biologist (Science & Survival), born in Brooklyn, New York
May 28 Gerald Cash, Gov-Gen (Bahamas)
May 28 Marshall Reed, Englewood California, actor (Fred Asher-Lineup)

May 29 John F. Kennedy, 35th US President (1961-1963) and Senator (D-Mass), born in Brookline, Massachusetts (d. 1963)

June

Jun 1 William S. Knowles, American chemist, Nobel Prize laureate, (d. 2012)

Jun 2 Max Showalter, Caldwell Ks, actor/composer (Stockard Channing Show)
Jun 2 Heinz Sielmann, German photographer and filmmaker (d. 2006)

Jun 3 Leo Gorcey, American actor (Bowery Boys, Road to Zanzibar), born in NYC, New York (d. 1969)

Jun 4 Allen Greenwood, deputy CEO (British Aerospace)
Jun 4 Charles Collingwood, Mich, news commentator (CBS, Chronicles)
Jun 4 Howard Metzenbaum, (Sen-D-Ohio, 1974-)
Jun 4 Robert Merrill, American baritone (NY Metropolitan Opera), born in Brooklyn, New York

Jun 5 Carel van Dillen, resistance fighter

Jun 6 Kirk Kerkorian, American CEO and "father of the mega-resort" (MGM, UA), born in Fresno, California (d. 2015)
Jun 6 Prior Jones, cricketer (WI pace bowler in 9 Tests 1948-52)

Jun 7 Gwendolyn Brooks, US poet (Bean Eaters, Annie Allen, Pulitzer 1950)

Jun 7 Dean Martin [Dino Paul Crocetti], American singer and actor (Martin and Lewis, The Dean Martin Show), born in Steubenville, Ohio (d. 1995)

Jun 8 Byron R Whizzer White, Ft Collins, NFLer/Supreme Court Just (1962-93)

Jun 9 Eric J. Hobsbawm, Alexandria, Sultanate of Egypt, Marxist historian (The Age of Revolution; Capital; and Empire), (d. 2012)

Jun 10 William Barr, rector (Exeter College, Oxford)

Jun 11 James Bostock, painter/engraver
Jun 11 Joseph B Wirthlin, American businessmen, religious leader, member of the Quorum of the Twelve Apostles (LDS Church), born in Salt Lake City, Utah (d. 2008)

Jun 12 Priscilla Lane, American actress (Arsenic & Old Lace)

Jun 14 Al "Lash" LaRue, Gretna La, actor (Lash of the West, Wyatt Earp)
Jun 14 Atle Selberg, Norwegian mathematician

Jun 15 Al "Lash" La Rue, cowboy actor (Black Lash, Lash of the West)
Jun 15 Michalis Genitsaris, Greek singer and composer (d. 2005)

Jun 16 Katharine Graham, newspaper publisher (Washington Post), born in NYC, New York
Jun 16 Aurelio Lampredi, Italian mechanical engineer (Ferrari; d. 1989)
Jun 16 Irving Penn, American photographer

Jun 17 Atle Selberg, Norwegian mathematician (d. 2007)

Jun 18 Akhmet Jevdet Ismail Hajiyev, composer

Jun 18 Richard Boone, actor (Paladin-Have Gun Will Travel), born in Los Angeles, California
Jun 18 Arthur Tremblay, Canadian politician (d. 1996)

Jun 19 Joshua Nkomo, Zimbabwan minister (ZAPUA)

Jun 20 Igor Śmiałowski, Polish actor (d. 2006)
Jun 20 Ash Brownridge, American conservationist (National Wildlife Federation), creator of Ranger Rick, born in Toronto, Ontario (d. 2015)

Jun 23 Sid Watters Jr, horse trainer

Jun 26 William Hamilton, British MP

Jun 27 K M Rangnekar, cricketer (batted in 3 Tests India v Australia 1947-48)
Jun 27 Ronald George Hayward, political manager

Jun 28 Willem "Wim" Sonneveld, Dutch singer/actor (My Fair Lady)
Jun 28 Katherine Rawls, American swimming champion (d. 1982)

Jun 30 Lena Horne, American actress, singer (Stormy Weather, Wiz), born in Brooklyn, New York
Jun 30 Robert Vandekerckhove, Belgian politician
Jun 30 Susan Hayward, American actress (I Want to Live, Tulsa), born in Brooklyn, New York (d. 1975)

July
Jul 2 Pierre Dubois, Dutch literary

Jul 3 Helene Cordet, entertainer/nightclub owner
Jul 3 João Saldanha, Brazilian journalist and football manager (d. 1990)

Jul 4 Manolete, Spanish bullfighter (d. 1947)

Jul 5 Glenn Reeves, actor (Defending Your Life), born in Massillon, Ohio

Jul 6 Hugo Cole, composer and music critic, born in London (d. 1995)
Jul 6 Hugo Yarnold, cricketer (Worcestershire keeper & Test umpire)
Jul 6 Arthur Lydiard, New Zealand running coach (d. 2004)

Jul 7 Elton Britt, Marshall Ark, country singer (Sat Night Jamboree)
Jul 7 Lawrence F O'Brien, (Watergate conspirators broke into his office)
Jul 7 Fidel Sánchez Hernández, Salvadoran politician (d. 2003)
Jul 7 Woodrow Wilson "Red" Sovine, American country music singer, born in Charleston, West Virginia (d. 1980)

Jul 8 Faye Emerson, American actress (I've Got a Secret), born in Elizabeth, Louisiana (d. 1983)
Jul 8 Glenn Langan, actor (Amazing Colossal Man, Margie), born in Denver, Colorado
Jul 8 Pamela Brown, actress (Cleopatra, Beckett), born in London, England

Jul 9 Ted Steele, orchestra leader (Cavalcade of Stars), born in Hartford, Connecticut

Jul 10 Don Herbert, Waconia Minn, scientist/TV host (Watch Mr Wizard)
Jul 10 Reg Smyth, English cartoonist (Andy Capp)
Jul 10 Hugh Alexander, American baseball player (d. 2000)

Jul 12 Andrew Wyeth, Chadds Ford Pa, painter (Christina's World)

Jul 14 Arthur Leavins, violinist
Jul 14 Douglas Edwards, Alda Oklahoma, newscaster (CBS Evening News, FYI)

Jul 15 Robert Conquest, English historian and poet (The Great Terror), born in Great Malvern, Worcestershire (d. 2015)

Jul 16 William Bishop, actor (Steve-It's a Great Life), born in Oak Park, Illinois

Jul 17 Lou Bourdeau, baseball player/manager (1948 AP Athlete of Year)
Jul 17 Phyllis Diller, American comedienne and actress (Boy, Did I Get a Wrong Number), born in Lima, Ohio (d. 2012)
Jul 17 Kenan Evren, Turkish soldier and politician, (President of Turkey 1980-1989 by military coup), born in Alaşehir, Manisa Province (d. 2015)

Jul 18 Henri Salvador, French singer (d. 2008)

Jul 19 Robert Aitken, Zen co-founder (Diamond Sangha), born in Philadelphia, Pennsylvania
Jul 19 William W Scranton, (Gov-R-Pa), (d. 2013)

Jul 22 H. Boyd Woodruff, American microbiologist whose research led to antibiotics, born in Bridgeton, New Jersey (d. 2017)

Jul 23 Charles Kerruish, president (Tyndwald Isle of Man)
Jul 23 John Stokes, British MP (C), born in Sandy, Bedfordshire (d. 2003)
Jul 23 Kurt Kreuger, Swiss-German actor (Fear, Unfaithfully Yours), born in Michenberg, Germany (d. 2006)

Jul 24 John Hillaby, English writer and traveller
Jul 24 Robert Farnon, composer/conductor/arranger
Jul 24 Simon Slattvik, Norwegian cross country ski jumper (Olympic gold 1952)
Jul 24 Jack Moroney, Australian cricketer (d. 1999)

Jul 25 Whipper Billy Watson, Canadian professional wrestler (d. 1990)

Jul 26 Bertil Nordahl, Swedish soccer player (Olympic gold 1948)
Jul 26 Richard Desborough Burnell, England, double sculls (Olympic gold 1948)

Jul 27 John Cunningham, executive director (British Aerospace)
Jul 27 Moses Rascoe, blues Singer
Jul 27 Robert Cowans, executive director (British Aerospace)
Jul 27 Bourvil, French actor (d. 1970)

Jul 30 Eddy Grove, American actor, born in NYC, New York (d. 1995)

August
Aug 1 Benjamin Roberts, British industrial relations expert (London School of Economics) (d. 2011)

Aug 3 Jordan Whitfield, PA, actor (Swamp Fox) (d. 1967)

Aug 6 Robert Mitchum, actor (Winds of War, North & South), born in Bridgeport, Connecticut

Aug 11 Dik Browne, cartoonist (Hi & Lois, Hagar the Horrible)

Aug 12 Douglas Gunsekera, banker

Aug 13 Sid Gordon, American baseball player (d. 1975)

Aug 15 Jack Lynch, Irish politician, fourth Taoiseach, born in Shandon, Cork, Ireland (d. 1999)
Aug 15 Oscar Romero, El Salvador Roman catholic priest who was murdered, born in Ciudad Barrios, El Salvador (d. 1980)

Aug 16 Roque Cordero, Panama, composer (Sonata Breve)

Aug 17 Safa Khulusi, Iraqi writer and historian, born in Baghdad (d. 1995)

Aug 18 Casper Weinberger, US Secretary of Defense (1981-87)

Aug 22 John Lee Hooker, American blues guitarist (Boogie Chillen), born in Clarksdale, Mississippi (d. 2001)

Aug 23 Tex Williams, American country-western singer, born in Ramsey, Illinois (d. 1985)

Aug 24 Dennis James, wrestling announcer/TV host (PDQ), born in Jersey City, New Jersey

Aug 25 Mel Ferrer, American actor (Longest Day, Eaten Alive, 5th Floor), born in Elberon, New Jersey (d. 2008)

Aug 26 Jan Clayton, Tularosa NM, actress (Ellen Miller-Lassie)
Aug 26 William French Smith, Attorney General (1981-85)

Aug 27 Peanuts Lowrey, American baseball player (d. 1986)

Aug 28 Jack Kirby, American cartoonist (X-Men, Spider-Man, Hulk, Capt America), born in NYC, New York (d. 1994)

Aug 29 Isabel Sanford, American actress (Louise-Jeffersons/All in the Family), born in NYC, New York (d. 2004)

Aug 30 Denis Healey, English politician (Labour Chancellor of the Exchequer), born in London, (d. 2015)

September

Sep 2 Cleveland Amory, Nahant Mass, conservationist/TV reviewer (TV Guide)
Sep 2 Laurindo Almeida, Brazilian guitarist (developed bossa nova)

Sep 3 Eddie "Brat" Stanky, Phil Rizzuto's nemisis/2nd baseman (Dodgers)

Sep 3 Peter Winter, naval commander

Sep 4 Henry Ford II, American businessman and son of Henry Ford, (President of Ford Motor Company, 1945-79), born in Detroit, Michigan (d. 1987)

Sep 5 Jack Buetel, American actress (Outlaw, Half Breed), born in Dallas, Texas (d. 1989)

Sep 6 George Mann, English cricketer, born in Byfleet, Surrey, England (d. 2001)

Sep 6 Philipp von Boeselager, German Wehrmacht officer, failed assassin of Adolf Hitler, born in Bonn, Germany (d. 2008)

Sep 7 John Cornforth, Australian chemist, Nobel Prize laureate, (d. 2013)

Sep 9 Rolf Wenkhaus, German actor (d. 1942)

Sep 10 Franfo Fortini [Franco Lattes], Italian poet, born in Florence (d. 1994)

Sep 10 Miguel Serrano, Chilean author and diplomat

Sep 11 Ferdinand Marcos, President of the Philippines (1965-86), born in Sarrat, Ilocos Norte, Philippines (d. 1989)

Sep 11 Henderson Forsythe, Macon MO, actor (Crisis at Central High)

Sep 11 Jessica "Decca" Mitford, English author (American Way of Death), activist and one of the Mitford sisters, born in Gloucestershire (d. 1996)

Sep 11 Daniel Wildenstein, French art dealer and racehorse owner (d. 2001)

Sep 12 Seamas NacNeill, Classical physicist and piper, born in Glasgow (d. 1996)
Sep 12 Pierre Sévigny, Canadian military officer and politician, born in Quebec, Canada (d. 2004)

Sep 13 Jon Thorarinsson, composer
Sep 13 Robert Eugene Ward, composer (Pantaloon), born in Cleveland, Ohio

Sep 15 Richard Arnell, composer

Sep 17 Isang Yun, Korean-born German composer, born in Sancheong, Korea (d. 1995)
Sep 17 Lawrence Jacob, artist (Sanitarium), born in Atlantic City, New Jersey
Sep 17 Peter Bennett, actor (Leonides-Adv of Sir Lancelot), born in London, England

Sep 18 Alan Ande Anderson, opera director
Sep 18 Gerrit Borgers, literature
Sep 18 June Foray, American voice actress (Cinderella, Cindy Lou Who), born in Springfield, Massachusetts (d. 2017)

Sep 19 Joe Pasternak, Transylvania Hungary, producer (Spinout, Big City)

Sep 20 [Arnold] Red Auerbach, NBA coach/GM (Boston Celtic), born in Brooklyn, New York
Sep 20 Fernando Rey, [Arambillet], La Coruna Spain, actor (Matter of Time)

Sep 21 Phyllis Nicolson, British mathematician (d. 1968)

Sep 22 Peter Adams, actor (Alternative), born in Los Angeles, California

Sep 23 Imry Nemeth, Hungarian hammer thrower (Olympic gold 1948)

Sep 24 Colin Cowe, senior bursar (Magdalen College Oxford)
Sep 24 William Putnam Bundy, editor (Lvaggerier & Vagaries), born in London, England

Sep 25 Johnny Sain, American baseball player (d. 2006)

Sep 26 Réal Caouette, French Canadian politician (d. 1976)

Sep 27 Louis Auchincloss, Lawrence NY, lawyer/novelist (Watchfires)
Sep 27 William T. Orr, American television producer (d. 2002)

Sep 28 Michael [George] Somes, England, dancer (Royal Ballet)
Sep 28 Vaclav Kaslik, Czechoslovakia, opera composer/conductor

Sep 30 Buddy Rich, American jazz drummer and band leader (Buddy Rich Band-Away We Go), born in Brooklyn, New York (d. 1987)
Sep 30 Chung Hee Park, general/President of South Korea (1961-79), assassinated
Sep 30 Yuri "Petrovich" Lyubimov, USSR, director (Taganka)

October
Oct 1 René A de Rooy, Suriname/Antillian poet (Juancho Picaflor)

Oct 2 Francis Jackson, organist & master of Music/York minister
Oct 2 William Marshall, band leader (Pennsylvanians), born in Chicago, Illinois
Oct 2 Charles Drake, American actor (d. 1994)
Oct 2 Christian de Duve, Thames Ditton, Surrey, cytologist and biochemist (Nobel, 1974), (d. 2013)

Oct 4 Albert de Klerk, Dutch composer/conductor
Oct 4 Jan Murray, comedian (Treasure Hunt, Who Killed Teddy Bear), born in The Bronx, New York

Oct 5 Robert Adams, English sculptor

Oct 6 Fannie Lou Hamer, American civil rights activist (Freedom Summer, Student Nonviolent Coordinating Committee), born in Montgomery County, Mississippi (d. 1977)

Oct 7 Helmut Dantine, actor (Shadow of the Cloak), born in Vienna, Austria
Oct 7 June Allyson, actress (Till the Clouds Roll By, Vegas), born in The Bronx, New York

Oct 8 Danny Murtaugh, American baseball manager (Pittsburgh Pirates), born in Chester, Pennsylvania (d. 1976)
Oct 8 Hans Poser, German composer, born in Tannenbergsthal (d. 1970)
Oct 8 Billy Conn, American boxer, born in Pittsburgh, Pennsylvania (d. 1993)
Oct 8 Walter Lord, American author (A Night to Remember), born in Baltimore, Maryland (d. 2002)

Oct 9 Kusuo Kitamura, Japan, 1500m freestyle swimmer (Olympic gold 1932)

Oct 10 Ilona Ference, actress (Quatermass II, Star of My Night)
Oct 10 Thelonious Monk, Rocky Mount North Carolina, American jazz pianist and composer

Oct 11 Franz Alphons Wolpert, composer

Oct 12 Hans Bentz van den Berg, Dutch actor (Last Train), born in Blaricum, Netherlands (d. 1976)

Oct 13 Burr Tillstrom, puppeteer (Kukla, Fran & Ollie), born in Chicago, Illinois

Oct 15 Arthur Schlesinger Jr, Ohio, historian (1946 Pulitzer-Age of Jackson)
Oct 15 Jan Miner, actress (Crime Photographer), born in Boston, Massachusetts

Oct 16 Alice Pearce, American actress (d. 1966)

Oct 17 Marsha Hunt, actress (Jennifer-Peck's Bad Girl, Jigsaw), born in Chicago, Illinois
Oct 17 Martin Donnelly, cricketer (brilliant lefty bat for NZ post-war)
Oct 17 Sumner Locke Elliott, Australian-born American novelist (d. 1991)

Oct 20 Efrain Jonckheer, premier Dutch Antilles
Oct 20 Jean-Pierre Melville, director (A Cop), born in Paris, France
Oct 20 Ken Cranston, cricketer (England all-rounder captained once in 1948)

Oct 21 Dizzy Gillespie, [John B], jazz trumpeter, a creator of modern jazz

Oct 22 Joan Fontaine, British-American actress (Gunga Din, Ivanhoe, Rebecca), born in Tokyo, Japan (d. 2013)

Oct 23 Robert Bray, American actor (Corey-Lassie, Stagecoach West), born in Kalispell, Montana (d. 1983)

Oct 24 Marshall Goldberg, NFL halfback (Chicago Cardinals)

Oct 25 Lee MacPhail, American baseball manager and league executive, born in Nashville, Tennessee (d. 2012)

Oct 26 Mario Biaggi, American politician (Rep-D&R-NY, 1969-88), born in New York (d. 2015)

Oct 27 Jack Plimsoll, South African cricketer (South African lefty quick, 3-143 in only Test 1947), born in Kalk Bay, South Africa (d. 1999)
Oct 27 Oliver Tambo, South African anti-apartheid politician and co-founder (African National Congress), born in Nkantolo, Bizana, South Africa (d. 1993)
Oct 27 Augustine Harris, British Bishop of Middlesbrough, born in West Derby, Liverpool (d. 2007)

Oct 28 Jack Soo, American actor (d. 1979)

Oct 29 Eddie Constantine, US/French actor (Lucky Jo, It Lives Again)
Oct 29 Henry Carlsson, Swedish soccer (Olympic gold 1948)

Oct 30 Bobby Bragan, American baseball player
Oct 30 Nikolai Vasilievich Ogarkov, Soviet field marshal (d. 1994)

Oct 31 Erik Routley, English Congregational minister, composer and musicologist, born in England (d. 1982)
Oct 31 William H. McNeill, Canadian-born historian (Rise of the West), born in Vancouver, British Columbia (d. 2016)
Oct 31 Thomas Hill, Canadian actor

November
Nov 1 Clarence E Miller, (Rep-R-OH, 1967-)
Nov 1 Margaret Taylor Burroughs, US author/house painter (Black Queen)
Nov 1 Zenna [Chlarson] Henderson, American sci-fi author (Anything Box)

Nov 2 Durward Knowles, yachtsman (Olympic gold 1968-Bahamas), born in Nassau, Bahamas

Nov 4 Leonardo Cimino, Manhattan, New York, actor (V, Dune), (d. 2012)

Nov 5 Claus Adam, American composer and cellist (Juilliard Quartet), born on Sumatra, Indonesia (d. 1983)
Nov 5 Jacob Everaers, office clerk/resistance fighter
Nov 5 Jacqueline Auriol, French aviatrix (d. 2000)
Nov 5 Banarsi Das Gupta, Indian former Chief Minister of Haryana (d. 2007)

Nov 6 Edgar Whitcomb, American politician and Governor of Indiana (1969-73), born in Hayden, Indiana (d. 2016)

Nov 7 Andras Mihaly, composer
Nov 7 Howard Rumsey, American jazz musician (Lighthouse Cafe), born in Brawley, California (d. 2015)

Nov 11 Julien-Francois Zbinden, composer
Nov 11 [Dallas] Mack/McCord Reynolds, American sci-fi author (Earth War)

Nov 12 Joseph Coors, CEO (Adolph Coors Co Brewery)
Nov 12 Jo Stafford, Coalinga California, singer (You Belong to me, Never Smile Again)

Nov 13 Robert Sterling, American actor (George Kirby-Adv of Topper), born in New Castle, Pennsylvania (d. 2006)

Nov 15 Gerardus H de Bold, bishop of Breda (1962-67)

Nov 16 John Whiting, British dramatist/actor (Saint's Day)

Nov 17 Jack Lescoulie, TV host (Jackie Gleason Show), born in Sacramento, California

Nov 19 Indira Gandhi, 4th Prime Minister of India (1966-77, 1980-84), born in Allahabad India (d. 1984)

Nov 20 Max Georg Baumann, composer
Nov 20 Pam Henningen, [Cornelia CP Ingenegeren], Indonesian/Dutch dancer
Nov 20 Ram Gopal, Indies/English dancer (Blue Peter, Purple Plain)
Nov 20 Robert Byrd, US Senator (Democrat-WV, 1959-2010), majority leader and once the longest-serving Senator in history, born in North Wilkesboro, North Carolina (d. 2010)
Nov 20 Bobby Locke, South African golfer (d. 1987)

Nov 21 Sem Presser, Dutch press photographer

Nov 22 Jean-Etienne Marie, composer
Nov 22 Bridget Bate Tichenor (born Bridget Pamela Arkwright Bate), Mexican surrealist painter, born in Paris, France

Nov 23 Hugh Joseph Charles James L'Etang, medical writer

Nov 24 Richard Bilderback Hervig, composer
Nov 24 Rita Corita, [Hendrika Sturm], Dutch singer

Nov 27 "Buffalo" Bob Smith, TV host (Howdy Doody), born in Buffalo, New York
Nov 27 Tiny Rowland, [Roland Fuhrop], German/British owner (Observer)

Nov 28 Kees Schilperoort, Dutch radio/TV host
Nov 29 Merle Travis, Muhlenberg County KY, country singer (16 Tons) (d. 1983)

December
Dec 1 Marty Marion, baseball player (NL MVP 1944)
Dec 1 William Tracy, Pitts, actor (To the Shores of Tripoli)

Dec 2 Ezra Stone, American actor/producer (Henry Aldrich)

Dec 2 Sylvia Syms, American jazz singer (Hello Dolly, Dream Girl, Them There Eyes), born in Brooklyn, New York (d. 1992)

Dec 5 Simone Gallimard, publisher
Dec 5 Ken Downing, English racing driver (d. 2004)

Dec 6 Kamal Jumblatt, leader of the Lebanese Druze (d. 1977)
Dec 6 Irv Robbins, Canadian-American entrepreneur (d. 2008)

Dec 8 Rufo I Wever, Aruban pianist/composer (Ca'i Organ)

Dec 9 James Angleton, head of counterintelligence for the CIA (d. 1987)
Dec 9 James Rainwater, American physicist, Nobel laureate (d. 1986)

Dec 10 Sultan Yahya Petra, King of Malaysia (d. 1979)

Dec 12 Edward Firth Henderson, arabist

Dec 13 Dave Street, actor/singer (Broadway Open House), born in Los Angeles, California
Dec 13 John Hart, American actor

Dec 14 Elyse Knox, actress (Hit the Ice, Black Gold), born in Hartford, Connecticut
Dec 14 Wilf Ferguson, cricket leg-spinner (West Indian of post-WWII years)
Dec 14 June Taylor, American choreographer (d. 2004)

Dec 15 Shan-ul-Haq Haqqee, linguist and writer of Pakistan (d. 2005)

Dec 16 Arthur C. Clarke, English sci-fi author (2001: A Space Odyssey, Childhood's End), born in Minehead, England (d. 2008)
Dec 16 Nabi Bux Khan Baloch, Sindhi scholar

Dec 17 Louis Salvador Palange, composer

Dec 18 Ossie Davis, Cogdell GA, actor/playwright (Hot Stuff, Man Called Adam)

Dec 19 Graham Sharp, British ice skater (d. 1995)

Dec 20 David Bohm, American-born physicist, philosopher, and neuropsychologist (d. 1992)

Dec 21 Alicia Alonso, ballerina (American Ballet Theatre), born in Havana, Cuba
Dec 21 Andre Eglevsky, choreographer (Limelight)
Dec 21 Sophie Masloff, American politician

Dec 22 Andrew Fielding Huxley, physiologist (Nobel 1963), born in London, England (d. 2012)
Dec 22 Gene Rayburn, TV game show host (Match Game), born in Christopher, Illinois
Dec 22 Piet De Somer, Belgian rector (U of Leuven)

Dec 24 Kim Jong-suk, Wife of Kim Il-sung, mother of Kim Jung-Il, "The Heroine of the Anti-Japanese Revolution" (d. 1949)

Dec 26 Rosemary Woods, Nixon's secretary, keep her away from your tapes

Dec 27 Earl of Inchcape, English large landowner/industrialist (P&O)
Dec 27 Onni Palaste, Finnish writer

Dec 28 Ellis Clarke, president Trinidad & Tobago (1976-87)

Dec 29 Tom Bradley, Mayor of Los Angeles (D-1973-93), born in Calvert, Texas (d. 1998)

Dec 30 Nancy Coleman, actress (Edge of Darkness), born in Everett, Washington

Dec 30 Seymour Melman, American industrial engineer (d. 2004)

Famous Deaths
January

Jan 2 Edward B Tylor, English anthropologist, dies at 84Jan 6 Hendrik P G Quack, lawyer/economist (Bank of Neth), dies at 82

Jan 10 William "Buffalo Bill" Cody, American Wild West hunter and showman (Buffalo Bill's Wild West), dies at 70

Jan 16 George Dewey, U.S. Admiral of the Navy, won Battle of Manila Bay, dies at 79

Jan 17 Hendrik Goeman Borgesius, Dutch politician, dies at 70

Jan 25 Edwin Tyler, cricketer (slow-lefty played once for England 1896), dies

Jan 29 Evelyn Baring earl Cromer, English consul-general in Egypt, dies at 75

February

Feb 5 Paul Rubens, English musical comedy composer, (Miss Hook of Holland), dies at 41

Feb 5 Jaber II Al-Sabah, Emir of Kuwait (b. 1860)

Feb 6 Edouard A Drumont, French anti-semite journalist, dies at 72

Feb 9 Francis Allan, cricket bowler (lefty in 1879 Aust-Eng Test), dies

Feb 10 Emile Pessard, composer, dies at 73

Feb 10 John William Waterhouse, Italian-born artist (b. 1849)

Feb 11 Oswaldo Cruz, Brazilian physician (b. 1872)

Feb 13 Joel Angel, Russian musicologist/composer, dies at 48

Feb 15 Charles A van Ophuysen, Dutch orientalist, dies at 60

Feb 16 Octave Mirbeau, French writer (b. 1848)

Feb 17 Edmund Bishop, English secretary of Thomas Carlyle, dies at 70

Feb 18 Charles E Barber, US chief engraver (1879-1917), dies

March
Mar 6 Jules HPFX Vandenpeereboom, premier of Belgium (1899), dies at 73

Mar 8 Ferdinand von Zeppelin, Dutch count/air pioneer, dies at 78

Mar 18 William Shalders, South African cricket batsman (12 Tests 1895-1907), dies

Mar 25 Elizabeth Storrs Mead, American educator (b. 1832)

Mar 29 Fran Gerbič, Slovenian composer, dies at 76

April
Apr 1 Scott Joplin, ragtime composer (The Entertainer), dies at 48

Apr 7 Spyridon Filiskos Samaras, composer, dies at 53

Apr 9 Edward Thomas, poet, killed in WW I
Apr 9 James Hope Moulton, British scholar of Classical Greek (b. 1863)

Apr 14 Lew [Lejzer L] Zamenhof, Polish doc/linguist (Esperanto), dies at 57

Apr 18 Moritz F Freiherr von Bissing, gov-gen of Belgium (1914-17), dies at 73
Apr 18 Vladimir Serbsky, Russian psychiatrist (b. 1858)

Apr 24 Oskar Blumenthal, writer, dies

May
May 1 Jose E Rodo, Uruguayan writer (Motivos de proteo), dies

May 3 Norman Callaway, NSW bat, cricketer (207 in only FC innings), dies

May 11 Otto Adolf Klauwell, composer, dies at 66

May 17 Charles Brooke, 2nd White Rajah of Sarawak (1868-1917), dies at 87

May 20 Philipp von Ferrary, Italian philatelist (b. 1850)
May 20 Valentine Fleming, Scottish politician (b. 1887)

May 25 Leon Felix Augustin Joseph Vasseur, composer, dies at 72
May 25 Maksim Bahdanovič, Belarusian poet (b. 1891)

June
Jun 6 Iacob Moresianu, composer, dies at 59

Jun 12 Maria Teresa Carreno, composer, dies at 63

Jun 15 Kristian Birkeland, Norwegian physicist (b. 1867)
Jun 15 Lillian Bassman, Russian emigrant to America, photographer and painter (Harper's Bazaar), (d. 2012)

Jun 20 James Mason Crafts, US chemist, dies at 78

Jun 27 Gustav von Schmolle, German economist (Historical School), dies at 79

July

Jul 2 Herbert Beerbohm Tree, British actor and theatre manager (King John, Trilby), dies at 64

Jul 4 Johan H C Kern, Dutch linguist (Sanskreet), dies at 84

Jul 8 Tom Thomson, Canadian painter (b. 1877)

Jul 12 Fournier, Swiss/French postage stamp merchant/forger, dies

Jul 14 Octave Lapize, French cyclist (b. 1887)

Jul 16 Ludwig Philipp Scharwenka, German composer (Album Polonaise), dies at 70

Jul 21 Christopher J Forster, British RAF-pilot/capt, dies in battle

Jul 27 Emil Theodor Kocher, Swiss surgeon, Thyroid specialist (Nobel 1909), dies at 75

Jul 31 Charlie Finlason, cricketer (South Africa's 1st Test), dies
Jul 31 Francis Ledwidge, Irish poet (b. 1881)
Jul 31 Hedd Wyn, Welsh poet (b. 1887)

August

Aug 1 Frank Little, American labor organizer (lynched) (b. 1879)

Aug 3 Ferdinand Georg Frobenius, German mathematician (Frobenius–Stickelberger formulae), dies at 67

Aug 7 Squadron Commander E.H. Dunning, first pilot to land his aircraft on a moving ship. (b. 1891)

Aug 15 Thomas J. Higgins, decorated Union Army soldier (b. 1831)

Aug 20 JFW Adolf Ritter von Baeyer, German chemist (Nobel 1905), dies

Aug 30 Uritsky, leader of Petrogradse Czech, dies

September
Sep 5 Marian Smoluchowski, Polish physicist (b. 1872)

Sep 8 Charles Edouard Lefebvre, composer, dies at 74

Sep 11 Georges Guynemer, French WW I pilot, dies at 22

Sep 12 Eric Lundie, cricketer (WWI Test South Africa v England 1914), dies

Sep 20 Herbert Morris, Jamaican deserter in France, executed at 17

Sep 23 Werner Voss, German World War I pilot (b. 1897)

Sep 25 Thomas Ashe, Irish revolutionary (b. 1885)

Sep 27 Edgar H G Degas, French impressionist artist (ballerina), dies at 83

October
Oct 9 Hussain Kamil, sultan of Egypt (1914-17), dies at 63

Oct 11 Harry Trott, cricketer (Aust capt played 24 Tests 1888-1898), dies

Oct 13 Florence La Badie, American actress

Oct 15 Mata Hari [Margaretha Geertruida Zelle], Dutch dancer and convicted German spy, executed by firing squad at 41

Oct 17 Maria J "Marie" Bakker, actress/wife of Maarten Stranger, dies at 59

Oct 22 Bob Fitzsimmons, English boxer (b. 1863)

Oct 27 Arthur Rhys Davids, English pilot (b. 1897)

Oct 28 Prince Christian of Schleswig-Holstein-Sonderburg-Augustenburg (b. 1831)

November
Nov 3 Léon Bloy, French novelist and essayist (b. 1846)

Nov 8 Colyn Blythe, cricketer (2509 F-C wickets), dies at 38 during WW I

Nov 11 Liliuokalani [Lydia Kamaka'eha], last queen of Hawaii (1891-93), dies from a stroke at 79

Nov 13 Emile Durkheim, French sociologist (Le suicide), dies

Nov 14 William Smith, British deserter in France, executed at 20

Nov 17 Auguste Rodin, French sculptor (Baiser, Thinker), dies at 77

Nov 18 Henry Spiekman, social-democratic politician, dies at 43

Nov 19 Basil Grieve, cricketer (batted in 2 Tests England v South Africa 1889), dies

Nov 22 Teoberto Maler, German-born explorer (b. 1842)

December

Dec 7 Ludwig Minkus, Austrian ballet composer, dies at 91

Dec 8 Mendele Moykher Sforim, Russian writer (b. 1836)

1917 Calendar

January

Sun	Mon	Tue	Wed	Thu	Fri	Sat
	1	2	3	4	5	6
7	8	9	10	11	12	13
14	15	16	17	18	19	20
21	22	23	24	25	26	27
28	29	30	31			

February

Sun	Mon	Tue	Wed	Thu	Fri	Sat
				1	2	3
4	5	6	7	8	9	10
11	12	13	14	15	16	17
18	19	20	21	22	23	24
25	26	27	28			

March

Sun	Mon	Tue	Wed	Thu	Fri	Sat
				1	2	3
4	5	6	7	8	9	10
11	12	13	14	15	16	17
18	19	20	21	22	23	24
25	26	27	28	29	30	31

April

Sun	Mon	Tue	Wed	Thu	Fri	Sat
1	2	3	4	5	6	7
8	9	10	11	12	13	14
15	16	17	18	19	20	21
22	23	24	25	26	27	28
29	30					

May

Sun	Mon	Tue	Wed	Thu	Fri	Sat
		1	2	3	4	5
6	7	8	9	10	11	12
13	14	15	16	17	18	19
20	21	22	23	24	25	26
27	28	29	30	31		

June

Sun	Mon	Tue	Wed	Thu	Fri	Sat
					1	2
3	4	5	6	7	8	9
10	11	12	13	14	15	16
17	18	19	20	21	22	23
24	25	26	27	28	29	30

July

Sun	Mon	Tue	Wed	Thu	Fri	Sat
1	2	3	4	5	6	7
8	9	10	11	12	13	14
15	16	17	18	19	20	21
22	23	24	25	26	27	28
29	30	31				

August

Sun	Mon	Tue	Wed	Thu	Fri	Sat
			1	2	3	4
5	6	7	8	9	10	11
12	13	14	15	16	17	18
19	20	21	22	23	24	25
26	27	28	29	30	31	

Setptember

Sun	Mon	Tue	Wed	Thu	Fri	Sat
						1
2	3	4	5	6	7	8
9	10	11	12	13	14	15
16	17	18	19	20	21	22
23	24	25	26	27	28	29
30						

October

Sun	Mon	Tue	Wed	Thu	Fri	Sat
	1	2	3	4	5	6
7	8	9	10	11	12	13
14	15	16	17	18	19	20
21	22	23	24	25	26	27
28	29	30	31			

November

Sun	Mon	Tue	Wed	Thu	Fri	Sat
				1	2	3
4	5	6	7	8	9	10
11	12	13	14	15	16	17
18	19	20	21	22	23	24
25	26	27	28	29	30	

December

Sun	Mon	Tue	Wed	Thu	Fri	Sat
						1
2	3	4	5	6	7	8
9	10	11	12	13	14	15
16	17	18	19	20	21	22
23	24	25	26	27	28	29
30	31					

Look out for more books in the Series by Kerry Butters.